HENRIETTA FLUFFYBOTTOM

An Introductory Guide to Feathered Adventures with Chickens

Contents

1

Introduction to Keeping Chickens

Are you ready to embark on a captivating journey into the world of chicken keeping? "An Introductory Guide to Feathered Adventures with Chickens" is a must-have book for anyone interested in raising their own flock. From the basics of chicken care to picking the chicken that's right for you, this introductory guide provides all the essential information you need to raise healthy and thriving chickens.

Discover the joys of chicken keeping as you delve into the chapters filled with practical advice, expert tips, and valuable insights. Learn about selecting the right breed for your needs, incubating and hatching eggs, caring for chicks in their early days, understanding chicken behavior and social dynamics, and maintaining the well-being of your flock.

Immerse yourself in the fascinating world of different chicken breeds and their unique characteristics. Explore the rewards of chicken keeping, from the pleasure of gathering fresh and nutritious eggs to the therapeutic benefits of connecting with nature. Uncover the joy of companionship and the sense of self-sufficiency that comes with raising your own food.

Written in a clear and engaging style, this book is perfect for beginners and experienced chicken enthusiasts alike. Whether you dream of a backyard flock for eggs or meat, seek a source of entertainment and companionship, or wish to embrace a sustainable and self-sufficient lifestyle, "An Introductory Guide to Feather Adventures with Chickens" is your ultimate companion on this exciting journey.

Get ready to experience the joys, challenges, and rewards of chicken keeping as you create a harmonious and thriving flock. Your chickens will thank you, and you'll find yourself immersed in a world of connection, fulfillment, and endless fascination. It's time to embrace the clucks, the fluffs, and the wonderful world of chickens.

2

Chapter One: Raising and Caring for Chickens

Introduction:

Congratulations on embarking on the journey of raising chickens! These delightful creatures can provide you with fresh eggs, natural pest control, and endless entertainment. In this chapter, we will cover the essential aspects of raising and caring for chickens, from selecting the right breed to providing them with proper housing, nutrition, and healthcare. Let's dive in!

Choosing the Right Breed:

Before bringing home your chickens, it's important to select a breed that suits your needs and preferences. Some common considerations include the breed's temperament, egg-laying capabilities, climate adaptability, and space requirements. Popular choices for backyard flocks include Rhode Island Reds, Sussex, Plymouth Rocks, and Leghorns. Research different breeds and select the ones that align with your goals and circumstances.

Housing and Space Requirements:

Providing your chickens with a safe and comfortable coop is crucial. The coop should protect them from predators, provide adequate ventilation, and offer enough space for each bird. As a general guideline, allow at least 4 square feet per chicken inside the coop and 8-10 square feet per chicken in the outdoor run. Ensure the coop has roosting perches, nesting boxes, and easy access for cleaning.

Feeding and Nutrition:

A well-balanced diet is essential for the health and productivity of your chickens. A typical diet for laying hens consists of commercial poultry feed, which contains a balanced mix of grains, protein, minerals, and vitamins. You can supplement their diet with kitchen scraps, vegetables, fruits, and occasional treats like mealworms. Ensure they always have access to fresh, clean water.

Daily Care and Maintenance:

Chickens require regular care and attention to thrive. Some key tasks include:

a. Checking on them daily: Observe your chickens daily to ensure they are active, eating, and behaving normally. Look for any signs of illness or distress.

b. Egg collection: Collect eggs daily to maintain their freshness. Inspect them for cracks or abnormalities.

c. Cleaning the coop: Regularly clean the coop by removing soiled bedding, replacing it with fresh material, and disinfecting the coop periodically.

d. Grooming and health checks: Inspect your chickens for signs of parasites, such as lice or mites, and treat them promptly if necessary. Trim their nails and beaks as needed.

Protecting Against Predators:

Chickens are vulnerable to a variety of predators, including raccoons, foxes, snakes, and birds of prey. Ensure your coop has secure fencing and sturdy locks to keep predators out. Consider burying wire mesh around the perimeter to prevent digging. Providing adequate lighting around the coop can also deter nocturnal predators.

Health and Disease Prevention:

Maintaining the health of your flock is crucial. Take the following measures to prevent diseases and keep your chickens in good shape:

a. Vaccinations: Consult with a veterinarian or local agricultural extension office to determine if vaccinations are recommended in your area.

b. Biosecurity: Limit visitors to your flock, quarantine new chickens before introducing them to the existing flock, and practice good hygiene to prevent the spread of diseases.

c. Regular health checks: Inspect your chickens for any signs of illness, such as changes in appetite, feather loss, or abnormal behavior. Consult a veterinarian if you notice any concerns.

Conclusion:

Raising and keeping chickens can be a rewarding and enjoyable experience. By selecting the right breed, providing proper housing, nutrition, and healthcare, and taking necessary precautions against predators and diseases, you can ensure the well-being of your feathered friends. In the next chapter, we will explore the fascinating world of egg incubation and hatching.

3

Chapter Two: Egg Incubation and Hatching

Introduction:

The process of egg incubation and hatching is a fascinating aspect of raising chickens. By incubating fertile eggs, you have the opportunity to witness the miracle of life as the chicks hatch and begin their journey. In this chapter, we will explore the essential steps and considerations for successful egg incubation and hatching. Let's get started!

Selecting Fertilized Eggs:

To begin the incubation process, you need fertilized eggs. If you have a rooster in your flock, chances are the eggs will be fertilized. Alternatively, you can purchase fertilized eggs from local breeders or hatcheries. Ensure the eggs are clean, of good quality, and not more than 10 days old.

Preparing the Incubator:

An incubator provides the controlled environment necessary for the development of the embryos inside the eggs. Follow these steps to prepare your incubator:

a. Cleanliness: Thoroughly clean the incubator and ensure it is free from dirt, dust, and any contaminants.

b. Temperature and humidity: Set the temperature and humidity levels according to the specific requirements of the breed you are incubating. Typically, the temperature should be around 99.5°F (37.5°C), and humidity should be maintained at 50-55% until the final three days, when it should be raised to 65%.

c. Calibration: Use a reliable thermometer and hygrometer to calibrate and verify the temperature and humidity readings inside the incubator.

Incubation Process:

Now that your incubator is ready, it's time to begin the incubation process:

a. Egg positioning: Place the eggs in the incubator with the pointed end slightly downward. This helps the embryo orient itself correctly for hatching.

b. Turning the eggs: Eggs need to be turned regularly to prevent the embryo from sticking to the shell and promote even development. Automatic incubators have built-in turners, while manual turning requires rotating the eggs 180 degrees three to five times a day. Stop turning the eggs three days before the expected hatch date.

c. Monitoring temperature and humidity: Regularly monitor the temperature and humidity inside the incubator to ensure they remain within the required range. Make adjustments as necessary to maintain optimal conditions.

Candling:

Candling is the process of examining the developing embryo inside the egg using a bright light source. It allows you to monitor the growth and development of the embryos and identify any potential issues or non-viable eggs. Candling should be done around day 7 and day 14 of incubation.

Hatching:

Hatching is an exciting and delicate phase of incubation. Here are some important points to consider:

    a. Increased humidity: Increase the humidity in the incubator to around 65% during the final three days of incubation to facilitate successful hatching. Avoid removing the lid of the incubator once hatching begins. Doing this can cause a decrease in humidity, causing the membrane in the egg surrounding the chick to 'shrink-wrap' around the chick inside. You want to avoid this.

    b. Pipping and hatching: Pipping is when the chick starts to break through the shell. Once a chick has pipped, avoid interfering or helping it <u>unless there are clear signs of distress</u>. Helping a chick to hatch does not make it weak or less likely to thrive. One must be very gentle if the decision is made to help the chick, however. Careful removal of small bits of the shell while avoiding blood vessels is necessary. Do more research on how to do this properly, if the decision is made to help a chick hatch. Hatching can take anywhere from a few hours to a couple of days.

    c. Post-hatch care: Once the chicks have hatched, leave them in the incubator for a few hours until they are all dry and active. Then, transfer them to a brooder with a heat source, food, and water.

Troubleshooting:

Incubation doesn't always go perfectly, and challenges may arise. Here are some common issues and their potential solutions:

    a. Low hatch rate: Check temperature and humidity levels, ensure egg quality, and address any potential equipment malfunctions.

    b. Stuck chick: If a chick is struggling to hatch, you may assist by gently peeling away bits of the shell. However, <u>extreme caution is necessary to avoid harming the chick.</u>

    c. Non-viable eggs: Remove any eggs that show no signs of development or have stopped growing.

Conclusion:

Egg incubation and hatching offer a captivating glimpse into the natural life cycle of chickens. By providing the right conditions, monitoring the process closely, and addressing any challenges that arise, you can experience the joy of seeing new life emerge from the eggs. In the next chapter, we will delve into the care and development of chicks in their early days.

4

Chapter Three: Care and Development of Chicks in Their Early Days

Introduction:

Congratulations on the arrival of your adorable new chicks! Whether they hatched at home or were purchased from a hatchery, these tiny creatures require proper care and attention during their early days. In this chapter, we will explore the essential aspects of caring for and fostering the healthy development of your chicks. Let's dive in!

Brooder Setup:

A brooder is a designated space where you will raise your chicks during their initial weeks. Here's how to set up a suitable brooder:

a. Size: Provide at least 2 square feet of space per chick initially. You can reduce the space as they grow.

b. Heat source: Maintain a consistent temperature of around 95°F (35°C) for the first week, gradually reducing it by 5°F (2.8°C) each week until reaching room temperature. A heat lamp or brooder plate can serve as the heat source.

c. Bedding: Use clean and absorbent bedding material, such as pine shavings or straw, to line the brooder. Avoid using newspaper or slick surfaces to prevent leg problems.

    d. Food and water: Place chick feeders and waterers in easily accessible locations within the brooder. Use shallow waterers to prevent drowning.

Temperature and Heat Regulation:

Maintaining the appropriate temperature is crucial for the well-being of your chicks. Keep the following points in mind:

    a. Temperature adjustment: Monitor the chicks' behavior to gauge their comfort. If they huddle together directly under the heat source, they may be cold and need more warmth. If they are excessively panting or moving away from the heat, they may be too hot and require a cooler area within the brooder.

    b. Heat source management: Position the heat source in a way that provides a warm zone and a cooler zone within the brooder. This allows the chicks to self-regulate their body temperature by moving closer to or farther away from the heat.

    c. Gradual temperature reduction: As the chicks grow, gradually reduce the temperature by adjusting the height of the heat source or decreasing the wattage of the heat bulb. Aim to reach room temperature by the fourth week.

Feeding and Watering:

Proper nutrition and hydration are vital for the healthy growth and development of your chicks. Consider the following:

    a. Starter feed: Provide a high-quality commercial chick starter feed specifically formulated for their nutritional needs. It should contain essential nutrients, including protein (18-20%) and vitamins.

    b. Feed availability: Ensure a constant supply of fresh feed in chick feeders. Monitor their intake and adjust the quantity as needed.

    c. Water provision: Clean and refill the waterers with fresh water daily. Make sure the waterers are not too deep, as chicks can drown.

d. Nutritional supplements: Consult with a veterinarian or poultry specialist regarding any necessary vitamin or electrolyte supplements to support the chicks' health.

Health and Hygiene:

Maintaining a clean and healthy environment is essential to prevent diseases and promote the well-being of your chicks. Here are some key points:

a. Clean bedding: Regularly clean the brooder by removing soiled bedding and replacing it with fresh material to prevent bacterial growth.

b. Regular observation: Observe your chicks daily for any signs of illness, abnormal behavior, or distress. Look for indicators such as lethargy, loss of appetite, respiratory issues, or diarrhea.

c. Preventing drafts: Avoid exposing the chicks to drafts or sudden temperature changes, as they are more vulnerable during their early days.

d. Handling and socialization: Gently handle the chicks to acclimate them to human contact. This fosters socialization and makes them more comfortable with human interaction as they grow.

e. If you have chicks inside your home, be aware that using pans coated with Teflon can lead to bird death if the pans are heated enough to release fumes.

Gradual Integration:

After a few weeks, your chicks will be ready to transition from the brooder to their permanent coop. Follow these steps for a smooth integration:

a. Acclimation period: Introduce the chicks to the outdoor environment gradually. Start by allowing supervised outdoor time during the day and gradually increase their exposure.

b. Coop preparation: Ensure the permanent coop is clean, secure, and properly ventilated. Provide appropriate roosting perches, nesting boxes, and access to food and water.

c. Integration with the flock: If you have existing adult chickens, introduce the chicks to the flock when they are fully feathered and similar in size. Monitor their interactions closely to prevent aggression or bullying.

Conclusion:

The early days of chick rearing are crucial for their healthy development and well-being. By providing a suitable brooder setup, maintaining proper temperature and heat regulation, ensuring nutritious feed and clean water, and prioritizing their health and hygiene, you set the foundation for thriving chickens. In the next chapter, we will delve into the fascinating process of chicken behavior and social dynamics within the flock.

5

Chapter Four: Chicken Behavior and Social Dynamics within the Flock

Introduction:

Understanding chicken behavior and the social dynamics within a flock is essential for creating a harmonious and thriving environment for your feathered friends. Chickens are social creatures with complex interactions and hierarchies. In this chapter, we will explore various aspects of chicken behavior, communication, and social structure, helping you gain insights into their world. Let's dive in!

Pecking Order:

Chickens have a hierarchical social structure known as the pecking order. This order determines the dominance and submission among flock members. Key points to consider:

a. Establishment: When new birds are introduced to the flock, they go through a period of establishing their place within the pecking order. This can involve minor aggression, posturing, and pecking as they establish their rank.

b. Dominant and submissive behaviors: Dominant chickens assert their authority through pecking, wing flapping, and chest bumping. Submissive chickens exhibit behaviors such as crouching, avoiding eye contact, and yielding to dominant individuals.

c. Stability: Once the pecking order is established, the flock dynamics tend to stabilize. However, it can be influenced by changes in flock composition or the introduction of new birds.

Communication and Vocalizations:

Chickens use various vocalizations and body language to communicate with one another. Understanding their communication cues can help you gauge their well-being and address any issues. Some common communication signals include:

a. Clucking: A soft and rhythmic clucking sound often indicates contentment and communication between hens.

b. Squawking: Loud squawking can indicate alarm, distress, or an attempt to assert dominance.

c. Crowing: Roosters crow to establish territory, communicate with other roosters, and announce their presence. And yes, hens will sometimes crow. Especially if there are no roosters around. One hen will assert dominance and try to fool any lurking predators into thinking there is a rooster around by crowing.

d. Body language: Observe their body postures, such as fluffed feathers (indicating relaxation) or erect feathers (indicating alertness or aggression).

Flock Bonding and Socialization:

Chickens are social creatures that establish bonds and form social groups within the flock. Consider the following:

a. Rooster roles: Roosters play a significant role in the flock dynamics. They protect the flock, communicate potential threats, and participate in courtship behaviors.

b. Hen interactions: Hens engage in activities such as foraging, dust bathing, and roosting together, fostering social bonds within the flock.

c. Chick integration: Introducing new chicks to an established flock should be done gradually to minimize aggression. Supervise the integration process and provide safe spaces for chicks to retreat if necessary.

Environmental Enrichment:

Providing a stimulating environment for your flock is beneficial for their well-being and helps prevent boredom and negative behaviors. Consider the following:

a. Foraging opportunities: Allow your chickens access to outdoor areas where they can scratch and forage for insects, worms, and vegetation.

b. Dust bathing areas: Provide a designated dust bathing area with dry soil or sand where chickens can engage in this natural behavior to maintain feather health and cleanliness.

c. Perches and roosting spots: Install perches at different heights in the coop to allow chickens to roost comfortably and establish their positions within the pecking order.

Managing Aggression and Conflict:

While some level of pecking and aggression is natural within a flock, excessive aggression can lead to injuries or stress. Consider these strategies for managing aggression:

a. Ample space: Provide enough space within the coop and run to minimize overcrowding, which can exacerbate aggressive behaviors.

b. Multiple resources: Ensure an adequate number of feeders, waterers, and nesting boxes to prevent resource guarding and reduce competition.

c. Diversion tactics: Provide distractions and environmental enrichment, such as hanging treats or introducing novel objects, to redirect aggressive behaviors.

Conclusion:

Understanding chicken behavior and the social dynamics within a flock allows you to create a harmonious and enriching environment for your chickens. By recognizing the pecking order, interpreting their communication cues, promoting flock bonding, providing environmental enrichment, and effectively managing aggression, you can foster a happy and cohesive flock. In the next chapter, we will explore common health issues in chickens and how to maintain their well-being.

6

Chapter Five: Common Health Issues in Chickens and Maintaining Their Well-being

Introduction:

Ensuring the health and well-being of your chickens is crucial for their overall vitality and productivity. Like any living creatures, chickens are susceptible to various health issues. In this chapter, we will discuss some common health problems that chickens may encounter and provide guidance on how to maintain their well-being. Let's dive in!

Prevention and Biosecurity:

Prevention is key to maintaining the health of your flock. Implement these practices to minimize the risk of disease:

a. Quarantine: When introducing new birds to your flock, quarantine them for a period of at least 30 days to monitor for any signs of illness or disease before integrating them with the existing flock.

b. Cleanliness: Keep the coop and surrounding areas clean, regularly removing droppings and soiled bedding. Proper sanitation helps prevent the buildup of harmful bacteria and parasites.

c. Biosecurity measures: Restrict access to your flock, limit contact with other poultry, and practice good biosecurity measures to prevent the introduction and spread of diseases. This includes disinfecting equipment and footwear, and avoiding contact with wild birds.

Common Health Issues:

a. Parasites: External parasites such as mites and lice, as well as internal parasites like worms, can cause discomfort, weight loss, and decreased egg production. Regularly inspect and treat your flock for parasites using appropriate medications.

b. Respiratory diseases: Common respiratory diseases in chickens include infectious bronchitis, Newcastle disease, and mycoplasma infections. Proper ventilation, minimizing stress, and practicing good biosecurity can help reduce the risk of respiratory diseases.

c. Egg-related issues: Problems with egg production can occur, such as soft-shelled eggs, egg binding (when an egg gets stuck inside a hen), or egg peritonitis (infection in the abdomen due to a ruptured egg). Ensure a well-balanced diet, sufficient calcium supplementation, and monitor the health of your hens to address such issues.

d. Coccidiosis: Coccidiosis is a common intestinal disease caused by a protozoan parasite. Maintain good hygiene, provide clean water, and consider preventive measures such as medicated feed or natural alternatives to control coccidiosis.

e. Injury and trauma: Chickens may experience injuries from predator attacks, fights within the flock, or accidental mishaps. Provide a safe and secure environment, promptly address any injuries or wounds, and separate injured birds if necessary.

Signs of Illness:

Being able to recognize signs of illness in chickens is crucial for early detection and prompt treatment. Look out for the following indicators:

a. Lethargy or weakness

b. Loss of appetite

c. Weight loss

d. Abnormal droppings (diarrhea, blood, or mucus)

e. Respiratory distress (coughing, sneezing, or nasal discharge)

f. Feather loss or abnormal feather appearance

g. Reduced egg production or abnormal eggs

h. Swollen or abnormal-looking eyes or beak

Veterinary Care and Medications:

Establish a relationship with a poultry veterinarian who can provide guidance and care for your flock. In cases of serious illness or outbreaks, consult a professional to obtain appropriate medications and treatments. Always follow the veterinarian's advice and adhere to recommended dosages and withdrawal periods.

Nutrition and Hydration:

Proper nutrition and hydration are vital for the overall health of chickens. Consider the following:

a. Balanced diet: Provide a high-quality commercial feed specifically formulated for the appropriate life stage of your chickens. Ensure it contains the necessary nutrients, including protein, vitamins, and minerals.

b. Access to fresh water: Clean and provide fresh water daily, ensuring it is easily accessible to all chickens. Water is essential for digestion, temperature regulation, and overall well-being.

Stress Management:

Stress can weaken the immune system and make chickens more susceptible to diseases. Minimize stressors by providing a comfortable and secure environment, maintaining consistent routines, avoiding sudden changes, and practicing gentle handling techniques.

Conclusion:

Maintaining the health and well-being of your chickens is vital for their productivity and happiness. By implementing preventive measures, monitoring for common health issues, recognizing signs of illness, providing proper nutrition and hydration, seeking veterinary care when needed, and managing stress, you can ensure a thriving flock. In the next chapter, we will explore different breeds of chickens and their unique characteristics.

Chapter Six: Exploring Different Breeds of Chickens and Their Unique Characteristics

Introduction:

The world of chicken breeds is diverse and fascinating, with each breed offering its own set of characteristics, appearances, and attributes. Whether you are interested in raising chickens for eggs, meat, or as beloved pets, understanding different breeds can help you choose the right fit for your goals and preferences. In this chapter, we will explore various popular chicken breeds, highlighting their unique characteristics and benefits. Let's begin our exploration!

Dual-Purpose Breeds:

Dual-purpose breeds are versatile chickens that are suitable for both egg production and meat. Some popular dual-purpose breeds include:

a. Rhode Island Red: Known for their exceptional egg-laying capabilities and vibrant reddish-brown feathers, Rhode Island Reds are hardy and adaptable birds.

b. Sussex: Sussex chickens are renowned for their docile nature, making them great choices for families. They produce good-quality eggs and have meat with excellent flavor.

c. Plymouth Rock: Also known as Barred Rocks, Plymouth Rocks are dependable layers and have a calm disposition. They have distinctive black and white barred feathers.

Egg-Laying Breeds:

If your primary focus is on egg production, these breeds are excellent options:

a. Leghorn: Leghorns are known for their exceptional egg-laying abilities, consistently laying large white eggs. They are active and prefer free-ranging.

b. Australorp: Originating from Australia, Australorps hold the record for the most eggs laid in a year. They are friendly, docile birds with glossy black feathers.

c. Orpington: Orpingtons are prized for their large brown eggs and gentle nature. They come in various colors, including black, blue, buff, and white.

Meat Breeds:

For those interested in raising chickens for meat production, consider these breeds:

a. Cornish Cross: Cornish Cross chickens are the most common breed used in commercial meat production. They grow rapidly and have a high meat-to-bone ratio.

b. Freedom Rangers: Freedom Rangers are a slower-growing meat breed, known for their flavor and ability to forage. They have a more natural and robust constitution compared to Cornish Cross.

Bantam Breeds:

Bantam chickens are smaller versions of standard-sized breeds and are popular for their compact size and ornamental value. Some notable bantam breeds include:

a. Silkie: Silkies are renowned for their fluffy plumage, which resembles silk. They have a calm and friendly temperament, making them popular as pets.

b. Sebright: Sebrights are small and charming birds known for their unique laced feathers and bright colors. They are popular exhibition birds.

c. Pekin: Pekin bantams, also known as Cochin bantams, have feathered legs and a calm demeanor. They are excellent broody hens and are often used as foster mothers for other chicks.

Fancy and Exhibition Breeds:

Fancy and exhibition breeds are bred for their unique and stunning appearances. They are primarily kept for ornamental purposes and exhibition shows. Some examples include:

a. Polish: Polish chickens are recognized for their distinctive crest of feathers on their heads. They come in various colors and have a lively and friendly disposition.

b. Frizzle: Frizzles have feathers that curl outward, creating a unique and eye-catching appearance. They are available in different breeds, such as Frizzle Cochins and Frizzle Silkies.

c. Serama: Seramas are the smallest breed of chickens, originating from Malaysia. They have a confident and active personality, making them popular pets.

Conclusion:

The world of chicken breeds is vast, offering a wide array of choices to suit different purposes and preferences. Whether you seek dual-purpose breeds, prolific egg layers, meat production breeds, bantams, or fancy exhibition birds, understanding their unique characteristics can help you make informed decisions. Take the time to research and consider the specific traits and requirements of each breed to ensure a successful and enjoyable chicken-raising experience. In the next chapter, we will explore further tips and considerations for raising and maintaining a healthy and thriving flock.

8

Chapter Seven: Further Tips and Considerations for Raising and Maintaining a Healthy and Thriving Flock

Introduction:

Raising a healthy and thriving flock of chickens requires ongoing care, attention to detail, and a commitment to their well-being. In this chapter, we will explore additional tips and considerations that will contribute to the success of your chicken-raising journey. By implementing these practices, you can ensure a happy and productive flock. Let's delve into the details!

Provide Ample Space:

Chickens need enough space to move around comfortably. Overcrowding can lead to stress, disease transmission, and aggression. Provide at least 4 square feet of coop space per standard-sized chicken and ample room in the outdoor run or free-ranging area.

Maintain a Clean Environment:

Cleanliness plays a vital role in preventing disease and maintaining flock health. Regularly clean the coop, removing droppings, soiled bedding, and old feed. Replace bedding material as needed and disinfect the coop periodically to minimize bacterial and parasite buildup.

Practice Good Hygiene:

Practicing good hygiene is essential for both you and your chickens. Wash your hands thoroughly before and after handling chickens, especially if you have multiple flocks or come into contact with other poultry. This helps prevent the spread of diseases between flocks and minimizes the risk of zoonotic infections.

Keep Feed and Water Clean:

Provide clean and fresh water to your flock at all times, replacing it daily. Ensure the waterers are clean and free of algae or debris. Similarly, store chicken feed in a cool, dry place to maintain its freshness and prevent contamination by pests or mold.

Maintain a Balanced Diet:

Offer a balanced and nutritionally complete diet to your chickens. High-quality commercial feeds designed for the specific life stage of your birds are readily available. Supplement their diet with fresh fruits, vegetables, and occasional treats to provide variety and added nutrients.

Monitor Egg Production:

Regularly monitor your hens' egg production to detect any abnormalities or changes. A sudden decline in egg production or consistently abnormal eggs may indicate health issues that need attention. Consult a veterinarian if necessary.

Regularly Inspect and Handle Chickens:

Frequent observation and gentle handling of your chickens allow you to detect any signs of illness or injury. Get familiar with each bird's normal behavior, appearance, and body condition to quickly identify any deviations. Handle chickens calmly and carefully to minimize stress.

Practice Predator Control:

Implement predator control measures to protect your flock from potential threats. Secure the coop and run with sturdy fencing, burying it underground to deter burrowing predators. Use motion-activated lights, deterrent noises, and secure locks to prevent access to the coop. Regularly inspect the perimeter for signs of entry or damage.

Monitor Weather Conditions:

Be mindful of extreme weather conditions and their impact on your flock. Provide shade and adequate ventilation during hot weather to prevent heat stress. Insulate the coop and provide heat sources during cold weather to protect your chickens from frostbite and hypothermia.

Continual Learning and Adaptation:

Stay informed about the latest practices, research, and advancements in chicken husbandry. Join online forums, engage with local poultry groups, and read reputable sources to expand your knowledge. Be open to adapting your methods as new information arises.

Conclusion:

By implementing these further tips and considerations, you can raise and maintain a healthy and thriving flock of chickens. Providing ample space, maintaining cleanliness and hygiene, offering a balanced diet, monitoring egg production, handling chickens regularly, practicing predator control, being mindful of weather conditions, and continuing to learn and adapt will contribute to the overall well-being of your flock. In the next chapter, we will explore the rewards of chicken keeping and the joy they bring to our lives.

9

Chapter Eight: The Rewards of Chicken Keeping and the Joy They Bring to Our Lives

Introduction:

Keeping chickens goes beyond providing eggs or meat. It is a rewarding and fulfilling experience that brings joy, companionship, and a sense of connection to nature. In this chapter, we will explore the numerous rewards of chicken keeping and how these charming creatures can enrich our lives. Let's dive into the joys of chicken keeping!

Fresh and Nutritious Eggs:

One of the primary rewards of keeping chickens is the abundance of fresh, nutritious eggs. Few things compare to the satisfaction of gathering eggs from your own flock. Not only do homegrown eggs taste delicious, but they are also richer in nutrients, including omega-3 fatty acids and vitamins, compared to store-bought alternatives.

Connection with Nature:

Chicken keeping provides an opportunity to reconnect with nature. Observing chickens as they forage, scratch the ground, and engage in their natural behaviors can be a source of tranquility and appreciation for the natural world. It reminds us of the simple joys found in the rhythms of nature.

Therapeutic and Stress-Relieving:

Interacting with chickens has therapeutic benefits that can reduce stress and promote relaxation. Their gentle clucking, rhythmic scratching, and contented demeanor have a calming effect. Spending time with chickens can serve as a form of mindfulness, allowing us to slow down and find peace in the present moment.

Educational Opportunities:

Raising chickens provides valuable educational opportunities, especially for children. Children can learn about the life cycle, responsible animal care, and the importance of sustainable food production. By involving them in chicken keeping, we foster a deeper understanding and appreciation for where our food comes from.

Companionship and Entertainment:

Chickens have distinct personalities and can provide companionship and entertainment. Some breeds are naturally more curious and friendly, while others may be more independent. Watching their social interactions, amusing behaviors, and the way they communicate can bring joy and amusement to our daily lives.

Environmental Benefits:

Chickens offer environmental benefits as well. They can help control pests by consuming insects, slugs, and snails in your garden or yard. Their scratching and pecking also contribute to soil aeration and nutrient distribution, enhancing the health of the surrounding ecosystem.

Sense of Self-Sufficiency:

Keeping chickens fosters a sense of self-sufficiency and empowerment. By producing your own eggs or meat, you reduce reliance on commercial agriculture and have more control over the quality and source of your food. It can instill a sense of accomplishment and pride in providing for yourself and your family.

Community Engagement:

Chicken keeping can foster connections within the community. Sharing surplus eggs or even knowledge and experiences with fellow chicken keepers builds a sense of camaraderie. Participating in local poultry clubs, events, or workshops provides opportunities to learn from others and engage in a shared passion.

Teaching Responsibility and Care:

Caring for chickens teaches responsibility and compassion, particularly for younger members of the family. Children learn the importance of daily chores, such as feeding, watering, and collecting eggs. They develop empathy by nurturing and observing the needs of these gentle creatures.

Heartwarming Relationships:

Finally, chickens have the remarkable ability to form bonds with their human caretakers. While each chicken has its own personality, they can recognize their owners, show affection, and even enjoy human interaction. The relationships formed with these feathered friends can be heartwarming and bring immeasurable joy.

Conclusion:

The rewards of chicken keeping extend beyond the practical benefits of fresh eggs and pest control. Chickens bring joy, connection to nature, therapeutic value, educational opportunities, companionship, and a sense of self-sufficiency. They contribute to the richness of our lives, fostering a deeper appreciation for the wonders of the natural world. As you embark on your chicken-raising journey, may you embrace the many rewards and find fulfillment in the simple pleasures of tending to your flock.